The Passion of the

CHRIST

The Passion of the CHRIST

CLARE HAWORTH-MADEN
Editor

Saraband

Page 1: Christ on the cross, by Fra Angelico.

Page 2: Giotto's depiction of the fateful kiss of Judas.

Page 3: A detail from a Fra Angelico panel showing Christ being lifted from the cross.

Published by Saraband (Scotland) Limited, The Arthouse, 752–756 Argyle Street, Glasgow G3 8UJ, Scotland
hermes@saraband.net

ISBN: 1-887354-38-7

Printed in China

10 9 8 7 6 5 4 3 2 1

Acknowledgements
Extracts from the Authorized Version of the Bible (The King James Bible), the rights in which are vested in the Crown, are reproduced by permission of the Crown's Patentee, Cambridge University Press.

The publisher would like to thank the following people for their assistance in the preparation of this book: Deborah Hayes, Phoebe Wong. Grateful acknowledgment is also made for the illustrations featured in this book, which are reproduced courtesy of Planet Art, with the exception of the following:

© **2002 Arttoday.com, Inc:** 16, 18, 31, 32, 46, 47, 48, 49; **Saraband Image Library:** 14, 15, 21, 28, 29, 34, 38, 40, 41, 42, 44, 45, 50, 54, 57, 69, 71, 78.

Bibliography
Douglas, J. D. & Tenney, Merrill C., *NIV Compact Dictionary of the Bible*, Hodder & Stoughton, London, 1989.
Farmer, David, *Oxford Dictionary of Saints*, Oxford University Press, Oxford, 1996.
Fisher, Sally, *The Square Halo and Other Mysteries of Western Art*, Harry N. Abrams, Inc., New York, 1995.
Pawson, David, *Unlocking the Bible Omnibus*, Collins, London, 2003.
The Holy Bible, the King James Version.
The Lion Handbook to the Bible, Lion Publishing plc, Oxford, 1983.

CONTENTS

Introduction

For even hereunto were ye called: because Christ also suffered for us, leaving us an example, that ye should follow in his steps.

—PETER 2:21

The resignation with which Christ endured the most horrific of deaths in order to redeem humankind has awed Christians for over two millennia. And while martyrs have literally followed in His steps, Christ's example has inspired many ordinary people to find the courage to bear their sufferings in this world in the hope of being rewarded with everlasting life in the next.

The Passion as Recounted in the Gospels

The terrible details of Christ's Passion (a word derived from the Church Latin *passio*, "suffering") following His triumphant entry into Jerusalem are described in each of the four gospels of the New Testament. Although they tell essentially the same tale, Matthew, Mark, Luke, and John's accounts vary slightly, maybe partly because they were writing for different audiences.

Matthew is believed to have been Matthew Levi, the tax-collector and one of Christ's twelve apostles, and it is likely that his gospel was aimed at Jews who had become Christians, just as he had. This is why he identifies Christ as the king of the Jews and long-awaited Messiah, as prophesied in the Old Testament.

Scholars have associated Mark with John Mark, a companion of Barnabas, Paul, and, most significantly, Peter, the first pope, on whose recollections the gospel is traditionally said to be based. The evangelical, action-packed tone of Mark's gospel, and emphasis on Christ being the "son of man," suggests that it was targeted at Roman Gentiles whom he hoped to convert to Christianity. It is thought that Mark's gospel is the oldest, and that it was later expanded upon by Matthew and Luke.

Another associate of Paul was the physician Luke, a Syrian from Antioch, and probably the author of Luke's gospel. Luke states that his gospel is drawn from the reminiscences of "eyewitnesses, and ministers of the word" for Theophilus, "That thou mightest know the certainty of those things, wherein thou hast been instructed" (Luke 1:2–4). As well as being a historical testimony composed for an interested and educated Greek, Luke's gospel is evangelical in its portrayal of Christ as the "savior" of humankind.

"The disciple whom Jesus loved," "This is the disciple which testifieth of these things, and wrote these things," it is stated in John 21:20 and 21:24. The author of John's gospel is consequently one of the apostles who was closest to Christ, and in all likelihood the fisherman son of Zebedee. Although it is a first-hand account, John's gospel is more of commentary and interpretation than the previous three (whose similarity has caused them to be termed the "synoptic gospels"), and was almost certainly the last to be set down. It is clear that John's purpose in writing his gospel was to strengthen the faith of existing believers in the "son of God."

THE EVENTS OF CHRIST'S PASSION

The haunting story of Christ's Passion starts with Christ entering Jerusalem on a donkey, the sound of "Hosannas" ringing in His ears, yet in the knowledge that it is only a matter of days before He will be betrayed and crucified.

It continues with the Last Supper, which Matthew, Mark, and Luke—but not John—say was the Passover meal with which Jews commemorate the Exodus and their deliverance from the Babylonian slavery. Unleavened bread and

wine are ritually consumed, and it is on this occasion that Christ institutes the Holy Eucharist by telling His disciples that the bread is His body, and the wine, His blood, which will soon be broken and spilled. (Poignantly, just as Jews sacrifice a lamb for the Passover meal in memory of the lamb's blood that their forebears daubed on their doorposts to save their firstborns from God's vengeance on the Egyptians, so Christ is the "Lamb of God" who will be sacrificed for humanity's salvation.) At this meal, John tells us that Christ washes His disciples' feet as a demonstration of humility, but also identifies Judas as His betrayer and predicts Peter's triple denial.

With the conclusion of the Last Supper, Christ leads His disciples to the Garden of Gethsemane and asks Peter, James, and John to keep watch while He prays to God to protect and sanctify His followers. They fall asleep, but nothing can in any case prevent the arrival of Judas with a band of men charged with arresting Christ by the Jewish priests, officials, and elders, and his traitorous identification of Christ with a kiss.

Above: *Tintoretto's dramatic depiction of the Last Supper vividly evokes the occasion when Jesus first introduced His disciples to the sacrament of the Eucharist (which some Protestants call the "Lord's Supper").*

THE PASSION OF THE CHRIST

*Opposite: Christ's
agony on the cross was
a fate reserved only for
those who were deemed
to deserve the cruelest
form of punishment.*

Christ is seized and taken before Caiaphas, the high priest in charge of the Sanhedrin (the supreme Jewish council or court), whose politically motivated members are hostile to the accused. In the meantime, Peter, in fear of arrest himself, indeed denies Christ three times. Christ is pronounced guilty of blasphemy, which, under Jewish law, merits the death penalty, but with Judea under Roman rule, the Sanhedrin is not empowered to execute its verdict, which is why Christ is taken before Pontius Pilate, the Roman procurator, or governor. Luke alone testifies that Pilate sends Christ on to Herod Antipas (the governor of Christ's home province of Galilee who is visiting Jerusalem for the Passover festival), who returns Him to Pilate. All agree, however, that it is with Pilate that Christ's fate is sealed when He admits to being the "king of the Jews," which, as the Jews point out, is a treasonous assertion that an appointee of the Roman emperor cannot overlook ("If thou let this man go, thou art not Caesar's friend: whosoever maketh himself a king speaketh against Caesar." John 19:12.) Nevertheless reluctant to condemn Christ to death, Pilate offers to release either Him or the criminal Barabbas, in accordance with his Passover practice of pardoning a prisoner. But the Jews present call for Barabbas to be freed, and for Christ to be crucified, and Pilate has no option but to concede.

Christ's physical suffering now begins. He is stripped, beaten, crowned with thorns, garbed in a robe the color of royalty, and forced to hold a reed scepter as He is cruelly mocked. Then He is sent for crucifixion (only John asserts that He Himself carries the cross on which He will die, the other three gospels assigning that role to Simon the Cyrenian) at Golgotha, or Calvary. Crucifixion is an appalling form of torture and execution that the Romans reserved for the most despicable of criminals, and Christ's hands and feet are duly nailed to the cross and a sign is erected above His head that reads *Iesus Nazarenus Rex Iudaeorum*, the Latin for "Jesus of Nazareth, King of the Jews." After six hours, death mercifully releases Christ from His agony.

The story of Christ's mortal life ends with Joseph of Arimathea, a prominent Jew and covert Christian, begging Pilate for permission to remove Christ's body from the cross. Pilate agrees, and the corpse is wrapped in a linen shroud and laid in a nearby sepulcher. Yet three days later, the sepulcher is found empty, and the resurrected Christ reveals Himself to various of His initially incredulous disciples. His work on Earth done, Christ finally ascends to heaven to be at the side of His divine father.

THE AGONY AND THE ECSTASY

Although the gospels' harrowing accounts of Christ's Passion have the power to shock, move, and humble the most detached of readers, their impact on those who have dedicated themselves to Christ can be truly extraordinary. It is recorded, for example, that St. Francis of Assisi (1181–1226) developed stigmata—five wounds that correspond to those inflicted on Christ during His Passion—in 1224, the first documented instance of the phenomenon.

Another pious stigmatic was the German Augustinian nun Sister Anna Katharina Emmerich (1774–1824), an ecstatic who recounted her revelations from God to the German writer Clemens Brentano (1778–1842). These were first published in 1833 as *Das bittere Leiden unseres Herrn Jesu Christi. Nach dem Betrachtungen der gottseligen Anna Katharina Emmerich* (*The Dolorous Passion of Our Lord Jesus Christ According to the Meditations of the Blessed Anne Catherine Emmerich*), and continue to inspire the faithful.

There is also a religious order devoted to the Passion, the Congregation of the Barefooted Clerics of the Most Holy Cross and Passion of Our Lord Jesus Christ, which was founded in 1720 in Italy by St. Paul of the Cross (1694–1775) in response to a vision. In addition to making vows of poverty, charity, and obedience, Passionists swear that they will promote a devotion to Christ's Passion in others.

How Ordinary Christians Commemorate the Passion

Above: Botticelli's Lamentation over the Dead Christ *(c. 1490) is a tempera panel in the Alte Pinakothek in Munich, Germany.*

Christ's Passion is at the forefront of every practicing Christian's mind during Holy Week, which begins on Palm Sunday and culminates on Easter Sunday. On Palm Sunday, palm crosses are distributed among congregations in remembrance of Christ's entry into Jerusalem, when, according to John 12:12–13, the people hailed Christ with palm branches. Maundy Thursday is the day on which the disadvantaged are traditionally invited into churches to have their feet washed by priests in emulation of Christ's demonstration of humility at the Last Supper. And on Good Friday, the Christian Church mourns the crucifixion of Christ, His resurrection being celebrated two days later, on Easter Sunday.

A popular tradition of performing passion plays, in which members of the lay Christian community re-enact the tragic events of the Passion, developed during the Middle Ages in Europe. But because many gradually lost their pious purpose and developed into scurrilous, anticlerical farces, they were increasingly banned from the sixteenth century onward. One that has survived, however, has been performed by the Bavarian villagers of Oberammergau, in Germany, every ten years since 1634, in accordance with a vow made to God in the hope that they would thereby be spared the Black Death.

THE WAY OF THE CROSS

The fervent devotion that the Passion aroused in medieval Christians remains alive today, often being reinforced by the Roman Catholic medium of the Way of the Cross, also known as the Stations of the Cross, *Via Dolorosa*, or *Via Crucis*, a series of fourteen tableaux that portray aspects of Christ's agony, as follows.

Christ is condemned to death.
Christ carries his cross.
Christ falls for the first time.
Christ meets his mother.
Simon the Cyrenian carries the cross.
Veronica wipes Christ's face.
Christ falls for the second time.
Christ meets the women of Jerusalem.
Christ falls for the third time.
Christ is stripped.
Christ is nailed to the cross.
Christ dies on the cross.
Christ is taken down from the cross.
Christ is laid in the sepulcher.

Opposite and right:
While John reported that Jesus carried His own cross to the place designated for His crucifixion, the other three gospels relate that Simon the Cyrenian (opposite) bore the cross for Him.

The origin of the Way of the Cross can be traced back to St. Francis of Assisi, who traveled to Egypt in 1219 on a mission to convert the Saracen sultan to Christianity. Although the sultan refused to abandon Islam, he did grant the Franciscan order guardianship of the Holy Sepulcher in Jerusalem, the city having been under the sultanate's control since 1187. In 1342, the Franciscans' guardianship was extended to the Holy Places in Jerusalem, the ultimate place of pilgrimage for Christians, which few had any hope of visiting. In 1686, Pope Innocent XI permitted the Franciscans to mount representations of the Stations of the Cross in their churches, and decreed that meditating on each would merit an indulgence, a privilege that Pope Benedict XIII broadened to embrace all faithful Roman Catholics in 1726. Now represented in most Roman Catholic churches, the Way of the Cross therefore offers a spiritual pilgrimage to those who are unable to visit the Holy Places in person.

The Stations, whose number was standardized by Pope Clement XII in 1731, include certain events that are absent from the gospels, such as Veronica's wiping of Christ's face, causing His blood-stained image to be miraculously imprinted upon her cloth. Veronica was first mentioned in the fourth- to fifth-century "Gospel of Nicodemus," and a relic that is said to be her "veil" has indeed been preserved in St. Peter's in Rome since the eighth century. Historians nevertheless speculate that because *vera icona* is the Latin for "true image," Veronica's existence was invented to underline the relic's authenticity.

THE PAGES THAT FOLLOW

Over the following pages, selected extracts from all four gospels (drawn from the King James Version of the New Testament) narrate the inexorable course of Christ's Passion. But because each gospel differs in content and style, readers are urged to read Matthew, Mark, Luke, and John for themselves in order to gain the fullest possible picture of Christ's suffering.

"I Am Come a Light into the World"

CHRIST'S ENTRY INTO JERUSALEM

Previous page and below: Zechariah, the prophet to whom Matthew refers in verse 21:4, prophesied that the Messiah would enter Jerusalem riding on an ass (Zechariah 9:9), as portrayed below by Fra Angelico.

1   And when they drew nigh unto Jerusalem, and were come to Bethphage, unto the mount of Olives, then sent Jesus two disciples,

2   Saying unto them, Go into the village over against you, and straightway ye shall find an ass tied, and a colt with her: loose *them*, and bring *them* unto me.

3   And if any *man* say ought unto you, ye shall say, The Lord hath need of them; and straightway he will send them.

4   All this was done, that it might be fulfilled which was spoken by the prophet, saying,

5   Tell ye the daughter of Sion, Behold, thy King cometh unto thee, meek, and sitting upon an ass, and a colt the foal of an ass.

6   And the disciples went, and did as Jesus commanded them,

7   And brought the ass, and the colt, and put on them their clothes, and they set *him* thereon.

8   And a very great multitude spread their garments in the way; others cut down branches from the trees, and strawed *them* in the way.

9   And the multitudes that went before, and that followed, cried, saying, Hosanna to the Son of David: Blessed *is* he that cometh in the name of the Lord; Hosanna in the highest.

10   And when he was come into Jerusalem, all the city was moved, saying, Who is this?

11   And the multitude said, This is Jesus the prophet of Nazareth of Galilee.

12   And Jesus went into the temple of God, and cast out all them that sold and bought in the temple, and overthrew the tables of the moneychangers, and the seats of them that sold doves,

13   And said unto them, It is written, My house shall be called the house of prayer; but ye have made it a den of thieves.

14   And the blind and the lame came to him in the temple; and he healed them.

15   And when the chief priests and scribes saw the wonderful things that he did, and the children crying in the temple, and saying, Hosanna to the son of David; they were sore displeased,

16   And said unto him, Hearest thou what these say? And Jesus saith unto them, Yea; have ye never read, Out of the mouth of babes and sucklings thou hast perfected praise?

17   And he left them, and went out of the city into Bethany; and he lodged there.

—MATTHEW 21:1–17

CHRIST PREDICTS HIS CRUCIFIXION

1 And it came to pass, when Jesus had finished all these sayings, he said unto his disciples,

2 Ye know that after two days is *the feast* of the passover, and the Son of man is betrayed to be crucified.

—MATTHEW 26:1–2

"I CAME NOT TO JUDGE THE WORLD, BUT TO SAVE THE WORLD"

23 And Jesus answered them, saying, The hour is come, that the Son of man should be glorified.

24 Verily, verily, I say unto you, Except a corn of wheat fall into the ground and die, it abideth alone: but if it die, it bringeth forth much fruit.

25 He that loveth his life shall lose it; and he that hateth his life in this world shall keep it unto life eternal.

26 If any man serve me, let him follow me; and where I am, there shall also my servant be: if any man serve me, him will *my* Father honour.

27 Now is my soul troubled; and what shall I say? Father, save me from this hour: but for this cause came I unto this hour.

28 Father, glorify thy name. Then came there a voice from heaven, *saying*, I have both glorified *it*, and will glorify *it* again.

29 The people therefore, that stood by, and heard *it*, said that it thundered: others said, An angel spake to him.

30 Jesus answered and said, This voice came not because of me, but for your sakes.

31 Now is the judgment of this world: now shall the prince of this world be cast out.

32 And I, if I be lifted up from the earth, will draw all *men* unto me.

33 This he said, signifying what death he should die.

34 The people answered him, We have heard out of the law that Christ abideth for ever: and how sayest thou, The Son of man must be lifted up? who is this Son of man?

35 Then Jesus said unto them, Yet a little while is the light with you. Walk while ye have the light, lest darkness come upon you: for he that walketh in darkness knoweth not whither he goeth.

36 While ye have light, believe in the light, that ye may be the children of light. These things spake Jesus, and departed, and did hide himself from them.

Below: John (12:13) relates that the people of Jerusalem "took branches of palm trees" before going forth to meet Jesus. In Jewish belief, the lulav *("palm branch" in Hebrew) can symbolize God, as well as a righteous man (*tzaddik*).*

37 But though he had done so many miracles before them, yet they believed not on him:

38 That the saying of Esaias the prophet might be fulfilled, which he spake, Lord, who hath believed our report? and to whom hath the arm of the Lord been revealed?

39 Therefore they could not believe, because that Esaias said again,

40 He hath blinded their eyes, and hardened their heart; that they should not see with *their* eyes, nor understand with *their* heart, and be converted, and I should heal them.

41 These things said Esaias, when he saw his glory, and spake of him.

42 Nevertheless among the chief rulers also many believed on him; but because of the Pharisees they did not confess *him*, lest they should be put out of the synagogue:

43 For they loved the praise of men more than the praise of God.

44 Jesus cried and said, He that believeth on me, believeth not on me, but on him that sent me.

45 And he that seeth me seeth him that sent me.

46 I am come a light into the world, that whosoever believeth on me should not abide in darkness.

47 And if any man hear my words, and believe not, I judge him not: for I came not to judge the world, but to save the world.

48 He that rejecteth me, and receiveth not my words, hath one that judgeth him: the word that I have spoken, the same shall judge him in the last day.

49 For I have not spoken of myself; but the Father which sent me, he gave me a commandment, what I should say, and what I should speak.

50 And I know that his commandment is life everlasting: whatsoever I speak therefore, even as the Father said unto me, so I speak.

—JOHN 12:23–50

"Behold, the
Hour Cometh"

THE LAST SUPPER

Previous page and below: The Last Supper has been illustrated by many notable artists, including Titian (previous page) and Leonardo da Vinci (below), whose famous fresco captures the moment when Jesus shocks His disciples by stating that one of them will betray Him.

12 And the first day of unleavened bread, when they killed the passover, his disciples said unto him, Where wilt thou that we go and prepare that thou mayest eat the passover?

13 And he sendeth forth two of his disciples, and saith unto them, Go ye into the city, and there shall meet you a man bearing a pitcher of water: follow him.

14 And wheresoever he shall go in, say ye to the goodman of the house, The Master saith, Where is the guestchamber, where I shall eat the passover with my disciples?

15 And he will shew you a large upper room furnished *and* prepared: there make ready for us.

16 And his disciples went forth, and came into the city, and found as he had said unto them: and they made ready the passover.

17 And in the evening he cometh with the twelve.

—MARK 14:12–17

"Take, Eat; This Is My Body"

20 Now when the even was come, he sat down with the twelve.

21 And as they did eat, he said, Verily I say unto you, that one of you shall betray me.

22 And they were exceeding sorrowful, and began every one of them to say unto him, Lord, is it I?

23 And he answered and said, He that dippeth *his* hand with me in the dish, the same shall betray me.

24 The Son of man goeth as it is written of him: but woe unto that man by whom the Son of man is betrayed! it had been good for that man if he had not been born.

25 Then Judas, which betrayed him, answered and said, Master, is it I? He said unto him, Thou hast said.

26 And as they were eating, Jesus took bread, and blessed *it*, and brake *it*, and gave *it* to the disciples, and said, Take, eat; this is my body.

Right: Giotto's exquisite depiction of the Last Supper, a fresco painted c. 1304–06, shows a serene Jesus with the disciples who are "exceeding sorrowful."

27 And he took the cup, and gave thanks, and gave *it* to them, saying, Drink ye all of it;

28 For this is my blood of the new testament, which is shed for many for the remission of sins.

29 But I say unto you, I will not drink henceforth of this fruit of the vine, until that day when I drink it new with you in my Father's kingdom.

—MATTHEW 26:20–29

CHRIST WASHES THE DISCIPLES' FEET

2 And supper being ended, the devil having now put into the heart of Judas Iscariot, Simon's *son*, to betray him;

3 Jesus knowing that the Father had given all things into his hands, and that he was come from God, and went to God;

4 He riseth from supper, and laid aside his garments; and took a towel, and girded himself.

5 After that he poureth water into a bason, and began to wash the disciples' feet, and to wipe *them* with the towel wherewith he was girded.

6 Then cometh he to Simon Peter: and Peter saith unto him, Lord, dost thou wash my feet?

7 Jesus answered and said unto him, What I do thou knowest not now; but thou shalt know hereafter.

8 Peter saith unto him, Thou shalt never wash my feet.

Below: During the Last Supper, Jesus anticipated His death by comparing the bread and wine that He urged the disciples to consume with His body and blood, which would soon be broken and shed for the remission of humankind's sins.

Jesus answered him, If I wash thee not, thou hast no part with me.

9 Simon Peter saith unto him, Lord, not my feet only, but also *my* hands and *my* head.

10 Jesus saith to him, He that is washed needeth not save to wash *his* feet, but is clean every whit: and ye are clean, but not all.

11 For he knew who should betray him; therefore said he, Ye are not all clean.

12 So after he had washed their feet, and had taken his garments, and was set down again, he said unto them, Know ye what I have done to you?

13 Ye call me Master and Lord: and ye say well; for *so* I am.

14 If I then, *your* Lord and Master, have washed your feet; ye also ought to wash one another's feet.

15 For I have given you an example, that ye should do as I have done to you.

16 Verily, verily, I say unto you, The servant is not greater than his lord; neither he that is sent greater than he that sent him.

17 If ye know these things, happy are ye if ye do them.

18 I speak not of you all: I know whom I have chosen: but that the scripture may be fulfilled, He that eateth bread with me hath lifted up his heel against me.

19 Now I tell you before it come, that, when it is come to pass, ye may believe that I am *he*.

20 Verily, verily, I say unto you, He that receiveth whomsoever I send receiveth me; and he that receiveth me receiveth him that sent me.

Above: Luke (22:24) says that an argument broke out among the disciples during the Last Supper about "which of them should be accounted the greatest." John explains that by washing their feet, Jesus was teaching them about equality and humility.

—JOHN 13:2–20

CHRIST IDENTIFIES JUDAS AS HIS BETRAYER, AND PETER AS HIS DENIER

21 When Jesus had thus said, he was troubled in spirit, and testified, and said, Verily, verily, I say unto you, that one of you shall betray me.

22 Then the disciples looked one on another, doubting of whom he spake.

23 Now there was leaning on Jesus' bosom one of his disciples, whom Jesus loved.

24 Simon Peter therefore beckoned to him, that he should ask who it should be of whom he spake.

25 He then lying on Jesus' breast saith unto him, Lord, who is it?

26 Jesus answered, He it is, to whom I shall give a sop, when I have dipped *it*. And when he had dipped the sop, he gave *it* to Judas Iscariot, *the son* of Simon.

27 And after the sop Satan entered into him. Then said Jesus unto him, That thou doest, do quickly.

28 Now no man at the table knew for what intent he spake this unto him.

29 For some *of them* thought, because Judas had the bag, that Jesus had said unto him, Buy *those things* that we have need of against the feast; or, that he should give something to the poor.

30 He then having received the sop went immediately out: and it was night.

31 Therefore, when he was gone out, Jesus said, Now is the Son of man glorified, and God is glorified in him.

32 If God be glorified in him, God shall also glorify him in himself, and shall straightway glorify him.

33 Little children, yet a little while I am with you. Ye shall seek me: and as I said unto the Jews, Whither I go, ye cannot come; so now I say to you.

34 A new commandment I give unto you, That ye love one

another; as I have loved you, that ye also love one another.

35 By this shall all *men* know that ye are my disciples, if ye have love one to another.

36 Simon Peter said unto him, Lord, whither goest thou? Jesus answered him, Whither I go, thou canst not follow me now; but thou shalt follow me afterwards.

37 Peter said unto him, Lord, why cannot I follow thee now? I will lay down my life for thy sake.

38 Jesus answered him, Wilt thou lay down thy life for my sake? Verily, verily, I say unto thee, The cock shall not crow, till thou hast denied me thrice.

—JOHN 13:21–38

Christ Prays to God, the Father

32 Behold, the hour cometh, yea, is now come, that ye shall be scattered, every man to his own, and shall leave me alone: and yet I am not alone, because the Father is with me.

33 These things I have spoken unto you, that in me ye might have peace. In the world ye shall have tribulation: but be of good cheer; I have overcome the world.

* * *

1 These words spake Jesus, and lifted up his eyes to heaven, and said, Father, the hour is come; glorify thy Son, that thy Son also may glorify thee:

2 As thou hast given him power over all flesh, that he should give eternal life to as many as thou hast given him.

3 And this is life eternal, that they might know thee the only true God, and Jesus Christ, whom thou hast sent.

Below: *Knowing that His days on Earth were numbered, Jesus entreated God to protect His disciples, as well as "them also which shall believe on me through their word" (John 17:20).*

Above: John recounts that before making his way to the Garden of Gethsemane, Jesus raised His eyes to heaven and prayed to God, saying "I have finished the work which thou gavest me to do" (17:4).

4 I have glorified thee on the earth: I have finished the work which thou gavest me to do.

5 And now, O Father, glorify thou me with thine own self with the glory which I had with thee before the world was.

6 I have manifested thy name unto the men which thou gavest me out of the world: thine they were, and thou gavest them me; and they have kept thy word.

7 Now they have known that all things whatsoever thou hast given me are of thee.

8 For I have given unto them the words which thou gavest me; and they have received *them*, and have known surely that I came out from thee, and they have believed that thou didst send me.

9 I pray for them: I pray not for the world, but for them which thou hast given me; for they are thine.

10 And all mine are thine, and thine are mine; and I am glorified in them.

11 And now I am no more in the world, but these are in the world, and I come to thee. Holy Father, keep through thine own name those whom thou hast given me, that they may be one, as we *are*.

12 While I was with them in the world, I kept them in thy name: those that thou gavest me I have kept, and none

of them is lost, but the son of perdition; that the scripture might be fulfilled.

3 And now come I to thee; and these things I speak in the world, that they might have my joy fulfilled in themselves.

4 I have given them thy word; and the world hath hated them, because they are not of the world, even as I am not of the world.

5 I pray not that thou shouldest take them out of the world, but that thou shouldest keep them from the evil.

6 They are not of the world, even as I am not of the world.

7 Sanctify them through thy truth: thy word is truth.

8 As thou hast sent me into the world, even so have I also sent them into the world.

9 And for their sakes I sanctify myself, that they also might be sanctified through the truth.

10 Neither pray I for these alone, but for them also which shall believe on me through their word;

11 That they all may be one; as thou, Father, *art* in me, and I in thee, that they also may be one in us: that the world may believe that thou hast sent me.

12 And the glory which thou gavest me I have given them; that they may be one, even as we are one:

13 I in them, and thou in me, that they may be made perfect in one; and that the world may know that thou hast sent me, and hast loved them, as thou hast loved me.

14 Father, I will that they also, whom thou hast given me, be with me where I am; that they may behold my glory, which thou hast given me: for thou lovedst me before the foundation of the world.

15 O righteous Father, the world hath not known thee: but I have known thee, and these have known that thou hast sent me.

16 And I have declared unto them thy name, and will declare *it*: that the love wherewith thou hast loved me may be in them, and I in them.

—JOHN 16:32–33, 17:1–26

The Agony in the Garden of Gethsemane

"THE SON OF MAN IS BETRAYED INTO THE HANDS OF SINNERS"

36 Then cometh Jesus with them unto a place called Gethsemane, and saith unto the disciples, Sit ye here, while I go and pray yonder.

37 And he took with him Peter and the two sons of Zebedee, and began to be sorrowful and very heavy.

38 Then saith he unto them, My soul is exceeding sorrowful, even unto death: tarry ye here, and watch with me.

39 And he went a little further, and fell on his face, and prayed, saying, O my Father, if it be possible, let this cup pass from me: nevertheless not as I will, but as thou *wilt*.

Opposite and below:
Peter, James, and John fell asleep in the Garden of Gethsemane as the agonized Jesus prayed to God, who sent an angel (opposite). Below, Mantegna's The Agony in the Garden.

40 And he cometh unto the disciples, and findeth them asleep, and saith unto Peter, What, could ye not watch with me one hour?

41 Watch and pray, that ye enter not into temptation: the spirit indeed *is* willing, but the flesh *is* weak.

42 He went away again the second time, and prayed, saying, O my Father, if this cup may not pass away from me, except I drink it, thy will be done.

43 And he came and found them asleep again: for their eyes were heavy.

44 And he left them, and went away again, and prayed the third time, saying the same words.

Above: *According to Luke 22:44, Jesus suffered such psychological agony while praying to God in the Garden of Gethsemane that "his sweat was as it were great drops of blood falling down to the ground."*

45 Then cometh he to his disciples, and saith unto them, Sleep on now, and take *your* rest: behold, the hour is at hand, and the Son of man is betrayed into the hands of sinners.

46 Rise, let us be going: behold, he is at hand that doth betray me.

—MATTHEW 26:36–46

The Kiss
of Judas

JESUS IS BETRAYED

Previous page and below: Judas had told his armed escort that he would identify Jesus by greeting Him with a kiss. Jesus was in no doubt of the significance of the gesture: "Judas, betrayest thou the Son of man with a kiss?" (Luke 22:48).

43 And immediately, while he yet spake, cometh Judas, one of the twelve, and with him a great multitude with swords and staves, from the chief priests and the scribes and the elders.

44 And he that betrayed him had given them a token, saying, Whomsoever I shall kiss, that same is he; take him, and lead *him* away safely.

45 And as soon as he was come, he goeth straightway to him, and saith, Master, master; and kissed him.

—MARK 14:43–4[5]

CHRIST'S ARREST

"THEN CAME THEY, AND LAID HANDS ON JESUS"

Previous page:
Giotto's depiction of
the betrayal that led
to Christ's arrest.

Below: The servant's
ear is severed
(Matthew 26:51).

50 And Jesus said unto him, Friend, wherefore art thou come? Then came they, and laid hands on Jesus and took him.

51 And, behold, one of them which were with Jesus stretched out his hand, and drew his sword, and struck a servant of the high priest's, and smote off his ear.

52 Then said Jesus unto him, Put up again thy sword into his place: for all they that take the sword shall perish with the sword.

53 Thinkest thou that I cannot now pray to my Father, and he shall presently give me more than twelve legions of angels?

54 But how then shall the scriptures be fulfilled, that thus it must be?

55 In that same hour said Jesus to the multitudes, Are ye come out as against a thief with swords and staves for to take me? I sat daily with you teaching in the temple, and ye laid no hold on me.

56 But all this was done, that the scriptures of the prophets might be fulfilled. Then all the disciples forsook him, and fled.

—MATTHEW 26:50–56

CHRIST IS CONDEMNED AND DENIED

CHRIST IS BROUGHT BEFORE THE HIGH PRIEST CAIAPHAS

Previous page: The bound Jesus is depicted standing before Annas and his son-in-law, the high priest Caiaphas.

Below: While Jesus was in the presence of the high priest, Peter denied Him three times.

53 And they led Jesus away to the high priest: and with him were assembled all the chief priests and the elders and the scribes.

54 And Peter followed him afar off, even into the palace of the high priest: and he sat with the servants, and warmed himself at the fire.

55 And the chief priests and all the council sought for witness against Jesus to put him to death; and found none.

56 For many bare false witness against him, but their witness agreed not together.

57 And there arose certain, and bare false witness against him, saying,

58 We heard him say, I will destroy this temple that is made with hands, and within three days I will build another made without hands.

59 But neither so did their witness agree together.

60 And the high priest stood up in the midst, and asked Jesus, saying, Answerest thou nothing? what *is it which* these witness against thee?

61 But he held his peace, and answered nothing. Again the high priest asked him, and said unto him, Art thou the Christ, the Son of the Blessed?

62 And Jesus said, I am: and ye shall see the Son of man sitting on the right hand of power, and coming in the clouds of heaven.

63 Then the high priest rent his clothes, and saith, What need we any further witnesses?

64 Ye have heard the blasphemy: what think ye? And they all condemned him to be guilty of death.

65 And some began to spit on him, and to cover his face, and to buffet him, and to say unto him, Prophesy: and the servants did strike him with the palms of their hands.

—MARK 14:53–65

PETER DENIES CHRIST
THREE TIMES

55 And when they had kindled a fire in the midst of the hall, and were set down together, Peter sat down among them.

56 But a certain maid beheld him as he sat by the fire, and earnestly looked upon him, and said, This man was also with him.

57 And he denied him, saying, Woman, I know him not.

58 And after a little while another saw him, and said, Thou art also of them. And Peter said, Man, I am not.

59 And about the space of one hour after another confidently affirmed, saying, Of a truth this *fellow* also was with him: for he is a Galilaean.

60 And Peter said, Man, I know not what thou sayest. And immediately, while he yet spake, the cock crew.

61 And the Lord turned, and looked upon Peter. And Peter remembered the word of the Lord, how he had said unto him, Before the cock crow, thou shalt deny me thrice.

62 And Peter went out, and wept bitterly.

—LUKE 22:55–62

JUDAS COMMITS SUICIDE

1 When the morning was come, all the chief priests and elders of the people took counsel against Jesus to put him to death:

2 And when they had bound him, they led *him* away, and delivered him to Pontius Pilate the governor.

3 Then Judas, which had betrayed him, when he saw that he was condemned, repented himself, and brought again the thirty pieces of silver to the chief priests and elders,

4 Saying, I have sinned in that I have betrayed the innocent blood. And they said, What *is that* to us? see thou *to that.*

5 And he cast down the pieces of silver in the temple, and departed, and went and hanged himself.

6 And the chief priests took the silver pieces, and said, It is not lawful for to put them into the treasury, because it is the price of blood.

7 And they took counsel, and bought with them the potter's field, to bury strangers in.

8 Wherefore that field was called, The field of blood, unto this day.

9 Then was fulfilled that which was spoken by Jeremy the prophet, saying, And they took the thirty pieces of silver, the price of him that was valued, whom they of the children of Israel did value;

10 And gave them for the potter's field, as the Lord appointed me.

—MATTHEW 27:1–10

Opposite and below: Matthew tells us that when the Sanhedrin condemned Jesus to death, Judas was so overcome with remorse that he hanged himself (below) after flinging down the thirty pieces of silver, or blood money, that he had been paid for his betrayal (opposite).

CHRIST IS BROUGHT BEFORE PONTIUS PILATE

Below: After the Sanhedrin had sentenced Jesus to death for blasphemy, He was brought before Pontius Pilate on a charge of treason, His Jewish accusers telling Pilate, "We found this fellow perverting the nation, and forbidding to give tribute to Caesar, saying that he himself is Christ a King" (Luke 23:2).

11 And Jesus stood before the governor: and the governor asked him, saying, Art thou the King of the Jews? And Jesus said unto him, Thou sayest.

12 And when he was accused of the chief priests and elders, he answered nothing.

13 Then said Pilate unto him, Hearest thou not how many things they witness against thee?

14 And he answered him to never a word; insomuch that the governor marvelled greatly.

15 Now at *that* feast the governor was wont to release unto the people a prisoner, whom they would.

16 And they had then a notable prisoner, called Barabbas.

17 Therefore when they were gathered together, Pilate said unto them, Whom will ye that I release unto you? Barabbas, or Jesus which is called Christ?

18 For he knew that for envy they had delivered him.

19 When he was set down on the judgment seat, his wife sent unto him, saying, Have thou nothing to do with that just man: for I have suffered many things this day in a dream because of him.

20 But the chief priests and elders persuaded the multitude that they should ask Barabbas, and destroy Jesus.

21 The governor answered and said unto them, Whether of the twain will ye that I release unto you? They said, Barabbas.

22 Pilate saith unto them, What shall I do then with Jesus which is called Christ? *They* all say unto him, Let him be crucified.

23 And the governor said, Why, what evil hath he done? But they cried out the more, saying, Let him be crucified.

24 When Pilate saw that he could prevail nothing, but *that* rather a tumult was made, he took water, and washed

Above: Ecce homo! *After Jesus had been scourged, crowned with thorns, and garbed in a purple robe, Pilate presented Him to the chief priests and officers of the Sanhedrin with the words "Behold the man!" (John 19:5).*

Below: Pilate absolved himself symbolically of responsibility for "this just person's" death by publicly washing his hands.

his hands before the multitude, saying, I am innocent of the blood of this just person: see ye *to it.*

25 Then answered all the people, and said, His blood *be* on us, and on our children.

—MATTHEW 27:11–25

CHRIST IS HUMILIATED

CHRIST IS SCOURGED AND MOCKED

26 Then released he Barabbas unto them: and when he had scourged Jesus, he delivered *him* to be crucified.

27 Then the soldiers of the governor took Jesus into the common hall, and gathered unto him the whole band *of soldiers.*

28 And they stripped him, and put on him a scarlet robe.

29 And when they had platted a crown of thorns, they put *it* upon his head, and a reed in his right hand: and they bowed the knee before him, and mocked him, saying, Hail, King of the Jews!

Previous page and right: Mark (15:16–20) relates that Pilate had Jesus scourged, after which his soldiers led Jesus to their hall, or praetorium, *where they called "the whole band" together to mock and humiliate Him.*

Opposite, page 52, and page 53: The Roman soldiers placed a crown of thorns on Jesus' head, then seized the reed that they had thrust into His hand to symbolize a scepter and beat Him with it, as depicted by Titian (opposite) and Caravaggio (pages 52 and 53).

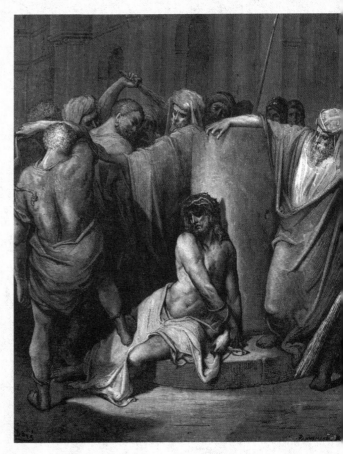

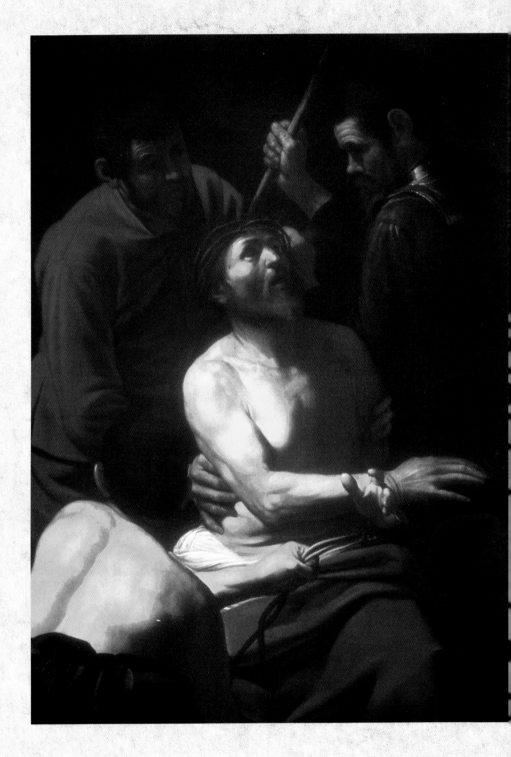

Below: The letters on the sign borne by the soldier in the illustration below stand for Iesus Nazarenus Rex Iudaeorum, *the Latin for the title* JESUS OF NAZARETH THE KING OF THE JEWS.

30 And they spit upon him, and took the reed, and smote him on the head.

31 And after that they had mocked him, they took the robe off from him, and put his own raiment on him, and led him away to crucify *him*.

32 And as they came out, they found a man of Cyrene, Simon by name: him they compelled to bear his cross.

—MATTHEW 27:26–32

Left: *Fra Angelico's fresco shows Christ wearing His crown of thorns and blindfolded. The artist has used a disembodied head and hands to portray Christ's humiliation symbolically rather than too graphically.*

CHRIST IS CRUCIFIED

THE CRUCIFIXION

33 And when they were come unto a place called Golgotha, that is to say, a place of a skull,

34 They gave him vinegar to drink mingled with gall: and when he had tasted *thereof*, he would not drink.

35 And they crucified him, and parted his garments, casting lots: that it might be fulfilled which was spoken by the prophet, They parted my garments among them, and upon my vesture did they cast lots.

36 And sitting down they watched him there;

37 And set up over his head his accusation written, THIS IS JESUS THE KING OF THE JEWS.

38 Then were there two thieves crucified with him, one on the right hand, and another on the left.

39 And they that passed by reviled him, wagging their heads,

40 And saying, Thou that destroyest the temple, and buildest *it* in three days, save thyself. If thou be the Son of God, come down from the cross.

41 Likewise also the chief priests mocking *him*, with the scribes and elders, said,

42 He saved others; himself he cannot save. If he be the King of Israel, let him now come down from the cross, and we will believe him.

43 He trusted in God; let him deliver him now, if he will have him: for he said, I am the Son of God.

44 The thieves also, which were crucified with him, cast the same in his teeth.

45 Now from the sixth hour there was darkness over all the land unto the ninth hour.

46 And about the ninth hour Jesus cried with a loud voice, saying, Eli, Eli, lama

Opposite: Raphael's panel shows Mary witnessing the agony endured by her son on the cross.

Below: Jesus died an excruciatingly painful death on His cross, which was placed between those of two thieves.

Below: Fra Angelico's depiction of the crucifixion.

sabachthani? that is to say, My God, my God, why hast thou forsaken me?

47 Some of them that stood there, when they heard *that*, said, This *man* calleth for Elias.

48 And straightway one of them ran, and took a spunge, and filled *it* with vinegar, and put *it* on a reed, and gave him to drink.

49 The rest said, Let be, let us see whether Elias will come to save him.

50 Jesus, when he had cried again with a loud voice, yielded up the ghost.

51 And, behold, the veil of the temple was rent in twain from the top to the bottom; and the earth did quake, and the rocks rent;

52 And the graves were opened; and many bodies of the saints which slept arose,

53 And came out of the graves after his resurrection, and went into the holy city, and appeared unto many.

54 Now when the centurion, and they that were with him, watching Jesus, saw the earthquake, and those things that were done, they feared greatly, saying, Truly this was the Son of God.

—MATTHEW 27:33–54

THE FINAL DESECRATION

31 The Jews therefore, because it was the preparation, that the bodies should not remain upon the cross on the sabbath day, (for that sabbath day was an high day,) besought Pilate that their legs might be broken, and *that* they might be taken away.

32 Then came the soldiers, and brake the legs of the first, and of the other which was crucified with him.

33 But when they came to Jesus, and saw that he was dead already, they brake not his legs:

34 But one of the soldiers with a spear pierced his side, and forthwith came there out blood and water.

35 And he that saw *it* bare record, and his record is true: and he knoweth that he saith true, that ye might believe.

36 For these things were done, that the scripture should be fulfilled, A bone of him shall not be broken.

37 And again another scripture saith, They shall look on him whom they pierced.

—JOHN 19:31–37

Below: In this woodcut by Albrecht Dürer, an angel collects the blood from Jesus' pierced side (John 19:34).

Left: *In Giotto's masterpiece* The Lamentation, *the angels and humans alike grieve for their beloved Jesus after He is deposed from the cross.*

Right: *In Raphael's expressive painting* The Deposition *(1507), the wound in Jesus' pierced side is clearly visible, along with the wounds to His hands and feet. The distraught Mary is faint with grief (far right).*

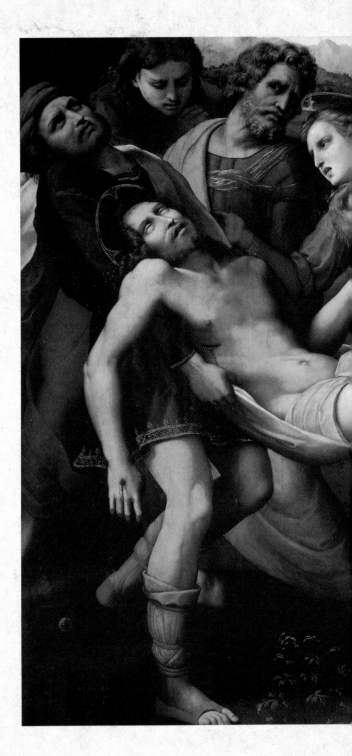

THE DEPOSITION AND ENTOMBMENT

Below, opposite, and overleaf: "Then they took the body of Jesus, and wound it in linen clothes" (John 19:40). Michelangelo, below; Caravaggio, opposite; and overleaf, Fra Angelico.

38 And after this Joseph of Arimathaea, being a disciple of Jesus, but secretly for fear of the Jews, besought Pilate that he might take away the body of Jesus: and Pilate gave *him* leave. He came therefore, and took the body of Jesus.

39 And there came also Nicodemus, which at the first came to Jesus by night, and brought a mixture of myrrh and aloes, about an hundred pound *weight*.

40 Then took they the body of Jesus, and wound it in linen clothes with the spices, as the manner of the Jews is to bury.

41 Now in the place where he was crucified there was a garden; and in the garden a new sepulchre, wherein was never man yet laid.

42 There laid they Jesus therefore because of the Jews' preparation *day*; for the sepulchre was nigh at hand.

—JOHN 19:38–42

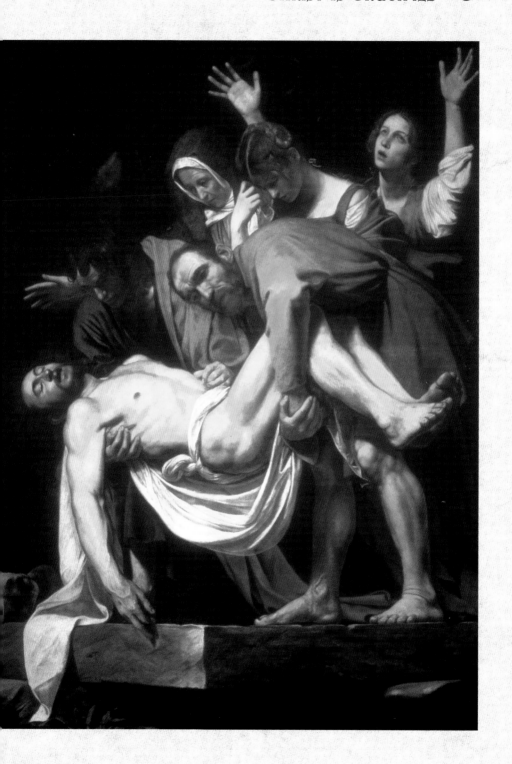

CHRIST IS RESURRECTED

THE RESURRECTION

1   Now upon the first *day* of the week, very early in the morning, they came unto the sepulchre, bringing the spices which they had prepared, and certain *others* with them.

2   And they found the stone rolled away from the sepulchre.

3   And they entered in, and found not the body of the Lord Jesus.

4   And it came to pass, as they were much perplexed thereabout, behold, two men stood by them in shining garments:

5   And as they were afraid, and bowed down their faces to the earth, they said unto them, Why seek ye the living among the dead?

6   He is not here, but is risen: remember how he spake unto you when he was yet in Galilee,

7   Saying, The Son of man must be delivered into the hands of sinful men, and be crucified, and the third day rise again.

8   And they remembered his words,

9   And returned from the sepulchre, and told all these things unto the eleven, and to all the rest.

10 It was Mary Magdalene, and Joanna, and Mary *the mother* of James, and other *women that were* with them, which told these things unto the apostles.

11 And their words seemed to them as idle tales, and they believed them not.

12 Then arose Peter, and ran unto the sepulchre; and stooping down, he beheld the linen clothes laid by themselves, and departed, wondering in himself at that which was come to pass.

—LUKE 24:1–12

Opposite: Fra Bartolommeo (1475–1517) painted this striking portrayal of the Risen Christ.

Below: "He is not here, but is risen!" (Luke 24:6), the angel told Mary Magdalene at the empty tomb of Christ.

NOLI ME TANGERE: "TOUCH ME NOT"

Below: Noli Me Tangere, *by Titian (c. 1511), shows Jesus apearing to Mary Magdalene, who was the first to see the resurrected Christ.*

11 But Mary stood without at the sepulchre weeping: and as she wept, she stooped down, *and looked* into the sepulchre,

12 And seeth two angels in white sitting, the one at the head, and the other at the feet, where the body of Jesus had lain.

13 And they say unto her, Woman, why weepest thou? She saith unto them, Because they have taken away my Lord, and I know not where they have laid him.

14 And when she had thus said, she turned herself back, and saw Jesus standing, and knew not that it was Jesus.

15 Jesus saith unto her, Woman, why weepest thou? whom seekest thou? She, supposing him to be the gardener, saith unto him, Sir, if thou have borne him hence, tell me where thou hast laid him, and I will take him away.

16 Jesus saith unto her, Mary. She turned herself, and saith unto him, Rabboni; which is to say, Master.

17 Jesus saith unto her, Touch me not; for I am not yet ascended to my Father: but go to my brethren, and say unto them, I ascend unto my Father, and your Father; and *to* my God, and your God.

18 Mary Magdalene came and told the disciples that she had seen the Lord, and *that* he had spoken these things unto her.

—JOHN 20:11–18

THE ROAD TO EMMAUS

13 And, behold, two of them went that same day to a village called Emmaus, which was from Jerusalem *about* threescore furlongs.

14 And they talked together of all these things which had happened.

15 And it came to pass, that, while they communed *together* and reasoned, Jesus himself drew near, and went with them.

16 But their eyes were holden that they should not know him.

17 And he said unto them, What manner of communications *are* these that ye have one to another, as ye walk, and are sad?

18 And the one of them, whose name was Cleopas, answering said unto him, Art thou only a stranger in Jerusalem, and hast not known the things which are come to pass there in these days?

19 And he said unto them, What things? And they said unto him, Concerning Jesus of Nazareth, which was a prophet mighty in deed and word before God and all the people:

20 And how the chief priests and our rulers delivered him to be condemned to death, and have crucified him.

21 But we trusted that it had been he which should have redeemed Israel: and beside all this, to day is the third day since these things were done.

22 Yea, and certain women also of our company made us astonished, which were early at the sepulchre;

23 And when they found not his body, they came, saying, that they had also seen a vision of angels, which said that he was alive.

Below: This etching by Gustave Doré shows Jesus with Cleopas and his companion on the road to Emmaus.

24 And certain of them which were with us went to the sepulchre, and found *it* even so as the women had said: but him they saw not.

25 Then he said unto them, O fools, and slow of heart to believe all that the prophets have spoken:

26 Ought not Christ to have suffered these things, and to enter into his glory?

27 And beginning at Moses and all the prophets, he expounded unto them in all the scriptures the things concerning himself.

28 And they drew nigh unto the village, whither they went: and he made as though he would have gone further.

29 But they constrained him, saying, Abide with us: for it is toward evening, and the day is far spent. And he went in to tarry with them.

Below: *In Titian's* The Supper at Emmaus, *the resurrected Jesus reveals Himself to the astonished company as He sat with them to dine.*

30 And it came to pass, as he sat at meat with them, he took
bread, and blessed *it*, and brake, and gave to them.

31 And their eyes were opened, and they knew him; and
he vanished out of their sight.

32 And they said one to another, Did not our heart burn
within us, while he talked with us by the way, and while
he opened to us the scriptures?

33 And they rose up the same hour, and returned to
Jerusalem, and found the eleven gathered together, and
them that were with them,

34 Saying, The Lord is risen indeed, and hath appeared to
Simon.

35 And they told what things *were done* in the way, and
how he was known of them in breaking of bread.

—LUKE 24:13–35

DOUBTING THOMAS

19 Then the same day at evening, being the first *day* of the
week, when the doors were shut where the disciples were
assembled for fear of the Jews, came Jesus and stood in
the midst, and saith unto them, Peace *be* unto you.

20 And when he had so said, he shewed unto them his
hands and his side. Then were the disciples glad, when
they saw the Lord.

21 Then said Jesus to them again, Peace *be* unto you: as *my*
Father hath sent me, even so send I you.

22 And when he had said this, he breathed on *them*, and
saith unto them, Receive ye the Holy Ghost:

23 Whose soever sins ye remit, they are remitted unto them;
and whose soever *sins* ye retain, they are retained.

24 But Thomas, one of the twelve, called Didymus, was not
with them when Jesus came.

25 The other disciples therefore said unto him, We have
seen the Lord. But he said unto them, Except I shall see

in his hands the print of the nails, and put my finger into the print of the nails, and thrust my hand into his side, I will not believe.

26 And after eight days again his disciples were within, and Thomas with them: *then* came Jesus, the doors being shut, and stood in the midst, and said, Peace *be* unto you.

27 Then saith he to Thomas, Reach hither thy finger, and behold my hands; and reach hither thy hand, and thrust *it* into my side: and be not faithless, but believing.

28 And Thomas answered and said unto him, My Lord and my God.

29 Jesus saith unto him, Thomas, because thou hast seen me, thou hast believed: blessed *are* they that have not seen, and *yet* have believed.

—JOHN 20:19–29

THE SEA OF TIBERIAS

1 After these things Jesus shewed himself again to the disciples at the sea of Tiberias; and on this wise shewed he *himself.*

2 There were together Simon Peter, and Thomas called Didymus, and Nathanael of Cana in Galilee, and the *sons* of Zebedee, and two other of his disciples.

3 Simon Peter saith unto them, I go a fishing. They say unto him, We also go with thee. They went forth, and entered into a ship immediately; and that night they caught nothing.

4 But when the morning was now come, Jesus stood on the shore: but the disciples knew not that it was Jesus.

5 Then Jesus saith unto them, Children, have ye any meat? They answered him, No.

6 And he said unto them, Cast the net on the right side of the ship, and ye shall find. They cast therefore, and now they were not able to draw it for the multitude of fishes.

7 Therefore that disciple whom Jesus loved saith unto Peter, It is the Lord. Now when Simon Peter heard that it was the Lord, he girt *his* fisher's coat *unto him,* (for he was naked,) and did cast himself into the sea.

8 And the other disciples came in a little ship; (for they were not far from land, but as it were two hundred cubits,) dragging the net with fishes.

9 As soon then as they were come to land, they saw a fire of coals there, and fish laid thereon, and bread.

10 Jesus saith unto them, Bring of the fish which ye have now caught.

11 Simon Peter went up, and drew the net to land full of great fishes, an hundred and fifty and three: and for all there were so many, yet was not the net broken.

12 Jesus saith unto them, Come *and* dine. And none of the disciples durst ask him, Who art thou? knowing that it was the Lord.

13 Jesus then cometh, and taketh bread, and giveth them, and fish likewise.

14 This is now the third time that Jesus shewed himself to his disciples, after that he was risen from the dead.

15 So when they had dined, Jesus saith to Simon Peter, Simon, *son* of Jonas, lovest thou me more than these? He saith unto him, Yea, Lord; thou knowest that I love thee. He saith unto him, Feed my lambs.

16 He saith to him again the second time, Simon, *son* of Jonas, lovest thou me? He saith unto him, Yea, Lord; thou knowest that I love thee. He saith unto him, Feed my sheep.

Above: *Christ revealed Himself to the disciples for the third time, in a scene depicted here by Raphael (1515),* The Miraculous Draught of Fishes.

17 He saith unto him the third time, Simon, *son* of Jonas, lovest thou me? Peter was grieved because he said unto him the third time, Lovest thou me? And he said unto him, Lord, thou knowest all things; thou knowest that I love thee. Jesus saith unto him, Feed my sheep.

18 Verily, verily, I say unto thee, When thou wast young, thou girdest thyself, and walkedst whither thou wouldest: but when thou shalt be old, thou shalt stretch forth thy hands, and another shall gird thee, and carry *thee* whither thou wouldest not.

19 This spake he, signifying by what death he should glorify God. And when he had spoken this, he saith unto him, Follow me.

20 Then Peter, turning about, seeth the disciple whom Jesus loved following; which also leaned on his breast at supper, and said, Lord, which is he that betrayeth thee?

21 Peter seeing him saith to Jesus, Lord, and what *shall* this man *do*?

22 Jesus saith unto him, If I will that he tarry till I come, what *is that* to thee? follow thou me.

23 Then went this saying abroad among the brethren, that that disciple should not die: yet Jesus said not unto him, He shall not die; but, If I will that he tarry till I come, what *is that* to thee?

24 This is the disciple which testifieth of these things, and wrote these things: and we know that his testimony is true.

—JOHN 21:1–24

CHRIST ASCENDS INTO HEAVEN

45 Then opened he their understanding, that they might understand the scriptures,

46 And said unto them, Thus it is written, and thus it behoved Christ to suffer, and to rise from the dead the third day:

47 And that repentance and remission of sins should be preached in his name among all nations, beginning at Jerusalem.

48 And ye are witnesses of these things.

49 And, behold, I send the promise of my Father upon you: but tarry ye in the city of Jerusalem, until ye be endued with power from on high.

50 And he led them out as far as to Bethany, and he lifted up his hands, and blessed them.

51 And it came to pass, while he blessed them, he was parted from them, and carried up into heaven.

52 And they worshipped him, and returned to Jerusalem with great joy:

53 And were continually in the temple, praising and blessing God. Amen.

—LUKE 24:45–53

Above and overleaf:
After appearing to the disciples for the last time (above: Bellini's Transformation of Christ*), Jesus ascended to Heaven on the third day (page 79: Raphael's* The Transfiguration*).*